"S. D. Ellison has given us a clear, concise, congenial (reader-friendly), crucial (it really does *matter*, doesn't it?) exposition of resurrection in the Old Testament testimony. Some may yammer, 'He doesn't discuss all the "critical" issues!' No, because (1) he doesn't want to bore us to tears and (2) he wants to 'put the cookies on the lower shelf' where all of us can enjoy them. A delightful read."
—**Dale Ralph Davis**
Former professor of Old Testament, Reformed Theological Seminary

"*Raised according to the Scriptures* helpfully highlights the fact that the gospel of Jesus Christ isn't an add-on to the Old Testament, but is written into its very fabric. S. D. Ellison highlights how the need for a death-defeating, resurrected rescuer is anticipated in multiple texts, preparing the way for the coming of the messiah in the New Testament. I'm sure that this book will be helpful to many in seeing Christ in all the Scriptures."
—**Gary Millar**
Principal, Queensland Theological College

"*Easter in the Old Testament?* If the Apostle Paul affirmed that Christ was raised 'according to the Scriptures,' we shouldn't be surprised by the subtitle of this accessible and engaging little volume! S. D. Ellison carefully considers the evidence for resurrection hope, tracing the subtle yet unmistakable 'precursors, promises, and prophecies' that permeate the Old Testament across its genres. Here is Easter in the Old Testament—'*as it is written*'!"
—**Sarah Dalrymple**
Tutor in Old Testament and Hebrew, Irish Baptist College

Raised according
to the Scriptures

Raised according to the Scriptures

Easter in the Old Testament

S. D. ELLISON

Foreword by Jason S. DeRouchie

WIPF & STOCK · Eugene, Oregon

For my nephews and nieces
Jude, Zach, Annie, Rosie, Caleb, Ben,
and those yet unborn.

I pray that each of you might find resurrection life in the good
news of Jesus Christ.

Contents

Foreword

"My God, my God, why have you forsaken me? . . . You lay me in the dust of death" (Ps 22:1, 15; cf. Matt 27:46). David was a prophet (Acts 2:30–31), and with these words he emphasizes God's absolute sovereignty in orchestrating the torment and termination of a royal figure (cf. Isa 53:10; Acts 4:27–28) whose hands and feet are pierced by evil mockers that cast lots for his garments (Ps 22:16–18; cf. Matt 27:28–29, 35). Yet through the horror comes healing, and through the terror and tribulation . . . triumph. As Isaiah would later declare, the very one whom God crushes, whose soul makes a substitutionary offering for guilt, will on the other side of slaughter see offspring, prolong his days, and carry out the purposes of God (Isa 53:10). Thus, David notes the slain sufferer crying to God, "You have rescued me. . . . I will tell of your name to my brothers" (Ps 22:21–22; cf. Matt 28:10). It is this foundational resurrection event that "all the ends of the earth shall remember," moving them to "turn to the Lord" (Ps 22:27). Indeed, "all the families of the nations shall worship" before God as testimony of this suffering but triumphant Lord's victory is "told . . . to the coming generation" and as his righteousness is proclaimed "to a people yet unborn" (Ps 22:27, 30–31). This man's resurrection would transform a global people forever. As God would testify through Isaiah, "By his knowledge shall the righteous one, my servant, make many to be accounted righteous, and he shall bear their iniquities" (Isa 53:11; cf. Rom 5:19).

Easter matters, and this is why I celebrate this little book, which unpacks some anticipations of Easter in the Old Testament. "If Christ has not been raised, your faith is futile, and you are still in your sins. Then those also who have fallen asleep in Christ have perished" (1 Cor 15:17–18). Without the resurrection, Jesus remains dead, which means we remain dead in our trespasses, alienated from God—without hope and without life (cf. Eph 2:4–7, 11–12). Every human needs to know and love this story, and this is why Ellison's *Raised according to the Scriptures* is a gift to Christ's church.

The resurrection of the dead is one of the fundamental truths of Christian teaching (Heb 6:1–2; cf. Mark 12:26; Luke 20:37). Indeed, Jesus's resurrection is the most important event in human history. All four Gospels testify to it (Matt 28:6–7; Mark 16:6; Luke 24:5–7, 34; John 20:8–10, 17–18), and the reality of Jesus's victory over the powers of darkness dominated all the preaching of the early church (Acts 1:22; 4:10, 33; cf. 1 Cor 1:23–24; 2:2).

In Adam, all humans become sinners (Rom 5:19), and because the wage of sin is death (Rom 6:23), "in Adam all die" (1 Cor 15:22; cf. Rom 5:12, 18). Yet Christ was no mere human, and his virginal conception meant that he was not in Adam, though he could stand as a substitute for those who were (Phil 2:6–8; Heb 2:14; 4:15; 5:2). "For our sake [God] made him to be sin who knew no sin, so that in him we might become the righteousness of God" (2 Cor 5:21). He was never a sinner who sinned but was instead perfectly holy, righteous, and obedient (Acts 3:14; Phil 2:8; 1 Pet 2:22; 1 John 2:1; 3:5). Therefore, although wicked men killed him, "God raised him up, loosing the pangs of death, because it was impossible for him to be held by it" (Acts 2:24; cf. 3:15; 4:10; 5:30; 13:30, 34, 37).

By his resurrection, Jesus was "vindicated by the Spirit" (1 Tim 3:16; cf. Isa 50:8) and "declared to be the Son of God in power" (Rom 1:4). Because of Jesus's obedience climaxing in the cross, God "highly exalted him and bestowed on him the name that is above every name" (Phil 2:8–9), thus giving him "all authority in heaven and on earth" (Matt 28:18; cf. Dan 7:13–14). In his death, Jesus received the punishment for our trespasses, but only in his resurrection did he secure our justification (Rom 4:25; cf. 1 Cor 5:21). His "one act of righteousness leads to justification and life for all men," for "by the one man's obedience the many will be made righteous" (Rom 5:18–19; cf. Isa 53:11). Because Jesus overcame the grave, believers' union with him in his death secures our union with him in his resurrection (Rom 6:5; 1 Cor 15:21–22; Eph 2:4–7; Phil 3:10; cf. Acts 4:2; 17:18, 32). Jesus's resurrection, therefore, gives us hope for lasting life and an inheritance that is imperishable, undefiled, and unfading (Acts 23:6; 24:15; Titus 3:7; 1 Pet 1:3–4). Hence, Jesus could declare, "I am the resurrection and the life. Whoever believes in me, though he die, yet shall he live" (John 11:25; cf. 1 Cor 15:22).

The Father is the one who raises the dead (John 5:21; cf. Acts 26:8), yet he does so through Jesus (John 6:39–40, 44, 54; cf. Matt 11:5; Luke 7:22). Out of his resurrection, Jesus proclaims light to the nations (Acts 26:23), and he does so by moving his disciples to declare his identity and work in the world (Acts 1:8; 13:46–47; cf. Matt 17:9; Mark 9:9; John 2:22). Thus, the Messiah's unparalleled victory leads to a universal mission of proclaiming hope for resurrection.

Leading up to the cross, Jesus stressed to his disciples how he must suffer, be killed, and rise on the third day (Matt 16:21; 17:23; 20:19; 26:32; 27:63; Mark 8:31; 9:31; 10:34; Luke 9:22; 18:33; John 2:19–20). We're told, however, that only after the resurrection did the disciples understand and believe these words *and* "the Scripture" (John 2:22; 12:16; 20:9). Where does the Old Testament speak of the Messiah's tribulation *and* triumph?

Following his resurrection, Jesus queried two of his disciples, "Was it not necessary that the Christ should suffer these things and enter into his glory?" Then Luke adds, "And beginning with Moses and all the Prophets, he interpreted to them *in all the Scriptures* the things concerning himself" (Luke 24:26–27, emphasis added). Later, Luke notes that Jesus opened the minds of his disciples "*to understand the Scriptures,* and he said to them, '*Thus it is written,* that the Christ should suffer and on the third day rise from the dead, and that repentance and forgiveness of sins should be proclaimed in his name to all nations, beginning from Jerusalem'" (24:45–47, emphasis added). Is this the message you find when you read the Old Testament? Luke records Paul noting something similar: "I stand here testifying both to small and great, saying nothing but *what the prophets and Moses said would come to pass*: that the Christ must suffer and that, by being the first to rise from the dead, he would proclaim light both to our people and to the Gentiles" (Acts 26:22–23, emphasis added). According to Paul "the gospel of God . . . concerning his Son" was "promised beforehand *through his prophets in the holy Scriptures*" (Rom 1:1–3, emphasis added). Indeed, it is this gospel that Paul emphasized is of "first importance":

> That Christ died for our sins *in accordance with the Scriptures*, that he was buried, that he was raised on the third day *in accordance with the Scriptures*, and that he appeared to Cephas, then to the twelve. Then he appeared to more than five hundred brothers at one time, most of whom are still alive, though some have fallen asleep. Then he appeared to James, then to all the apostles. Last of all, as to one untimely born, he appeared also to me. (1 Cor 15:3–8, emphasis added)

The saints of Jesus's day already had hope in the resurrection (John 11:24; cf. Matt 22:31–32; Mark 12:26; Luke 11:31–32; 14:14; 20:37–38; 24:26; John 5:29), and they associated this hope with the coming Messiah (Matt 11:4–6; Luke 7:22). This conviction grew out of the Old Testament's teaching. Thus, Paul was continually "testifying to the kingdom of God and trying to convince [his audience] about Jesus both *from the Law of Moses and from the Prophets*" (Acts 28:23, emphasis added).

The brief volume before you effectively shows many ways that Jesus's resurrection was indeed *according to the Scriptures* and that Easter is both indirectly foreshadowed and directly predicted in the Old Testament. Numerous precursors, promises, and prophecies of resurrection span the Law, Prophets, and Writings, and Ellison helpfully guides us through many of them. He points to several passages in Jesus's only Bible that magnify God's power to raise the dead, display this power in space and time, show righteous people hoping in life after death, and highlight direct prophecies of what can only be called future resurrection. Easter matters! I invite you to revel more in the gospel by considering how Jesus not only "died for our sins *in accordance with the Scriptures*" but was actually "raised on the third day *in accordance with the Scriptures*" (1 Cor 15:3–4, emphasis added).

—Jason S. DeRouchie, PhD
Research Professor of Old Testament and Biblical Theology
Midwestern Baptist Theological Seminary
Content Developer and Global Trainer
Hands to the Plow Ministries

Acknowledgments

THIS BOOK IS DEDICATED to my nephews and nieces. They are a constant source of joy to my wife, Tracy, and me. We love them, cherish them, and treasure the input we are privileged to have in their lives. Joyous life describes each of them. Above all our prayer is that each of them will hear the gospel with clarity, repent with sincerity, and live life in Jesus abundantly. Jude, Zach, Annie, Rosie, Caleb, Ben, and those yet unborn, I hope each of you will find resurrection life in the good news of Jesus Christ.

My wife, Tracy, reads virtually everything I write, listens to virtually everything I preach, and encourages me in virtually everything I do. She is devoted to me—a constant companion in love, life, and ministry. All of this I too frequently take for granted. For that I am sorry. I thank God afresh for you and continue to eagerly anticipate love, life, and ministry together.

I am grateful for a small group of people who willingly gave their time to read this book in its entirety: Elaine Colgan, Claire McNabb, Tom Moore, and Martin Parker. Their critiques improved its content and their encouragements kept me writing. I thank you all for your input to this project. I am also thankful to Matt Smethurst and The Gospel Coalition for permitting me to initially formulate these ideas in writing with my blog post "Anticipating Easter in the Old Testament." Jason DeRouchie delighted me with his willingness to write a foreword and kind words about the book; thank you for your encouragement.

As passionate as I am about the subject of this book, and the book's overarching goal of reclaiming the Old Testament as Christian Scripture, I recognize that it is niche. I am therefore indebted to Wipf and Stock for committing to the project. Matt Wimer and the team have been most helpful in initial conversations and throughout the process. It has been a pleasure to collaborate with you.

All the above are merely foretastes of glory divine, echoes of mercy, and whispers of love. I am a partaker in these blessings only because of the life, death, resurrection, and ascension of Jesus Christ. To him I owe my life, both now and in the age to come. This book, then, is offered as a further expression of my praise for my Savior whose story I tell—may its distribution be for the good of his people and to the glory of his name.

Introduction
The Power of the Subtle

CONFESSION: I AM A fan of *The Simpsons*.

I hope you are still reading. While I acknowledge that *The Simpsons* can be rude, offensive, and sometimes blasphemous, it also offers a razor-sharp social commentary on almost every aspect of life. Every time Ned Flanders appears I laugh at his absurdity and recoil at the reflection of myself in his Bible-believing Christian caricature. Sadly the caricature is often closer to reality than many Christians would like to admit. But what I really appreciate is the intelligence of the programme, often conveyed by subtle background jokes that could easily be missed. While largely incidental to the main story line, they enrich the program significantly—especially for regular viewers. Examples of these subtle jokes include Ned Flanders's sons Rod and Todd's football jersey numbers aligning to read 666 as they stand beside one another (one is wearing 66 and the other 6). It would have to be the Christian children wearing those numbers! Often it is the church sign. As it sits in the background of scenes it subtly communicates funny messages: "No Synagogue Parking," "Today's Topic: He Knows What You Did Last Summer," "God Welcomes His Victims," "Private Wedding: Please Worship Elsewhere." The character Homer is perhaps best-known for his catchphrase, "D'oh!"—in a delightfully subtle tribute his infant daughter is seen playing with a tub of "Play-(Annoyed Grunt)." These subtle jokes are a beautiful touch.

The power of these jokes is found in their subtlety. They would fail to elicit the same amusement if they were the main point in any given scene. The fact that they are mere background additions, which have been purposely placed, enhances the viewing experience. For the regular *Simpsons* viewer the sophisticated subtleties are a key part of the continued attraction. This is the power of the subtle.

The apostle Paul appears to have been a forerunner of sophisticated subtleties, which he in turn appears to have inherited from the Old Testament. Paul makes a striking and yet subtle statement about the resurrection in 1 Cor 15. True, a dead person being raised to life is not very subtle—it is striking. At the same time, this striking statement is delivered almost in passing—it is subtle. First Corinthians 15 is a lengthy chapter near the end of Paul's first letter to the Corinthian church in which he affirms extensively the reality and benefits of Jesus's resurrection. The striking subtlety is that Paul slips in that Christ was "raised on the third day *in accordance with the Scriptures*" (v. 4, emphasis added). For those familiar with their Bibles this might not, at first glance, appear all that remarkable. After all, Jesus frequently foretold his death and resurrection (Mark 8:31–33; 9:30–35; 10:32–40), the sermons in Acts repeatedly make mention of it (Acts 2:24–35; 4:2, 33; 13:32–37; 17:18, 32; 23:6; 24:15), and it looms large in the letters (Rom 1:4; 1 Cor 15; 2 Cor 4:14; Gal 1:1; Eph 1:20; Phil 3:10–11; Col 2:12; 1 Thess 1:10; 1 Pet 1:3). The resurrection is anything but subtle in the New Testament. The New Testament was not Paul's Bible, however.

When Paul tells the Corinthians that Jesus was raised according to the Scriptures, he is talking about what we now know as the Old Testament. And Paul is not alone. Jesus tells his disciples that "everything written about me in the Law of Moses and the Prophets and the Psalms must be fulfilled" (Luke 24:44). This undoubtedly includes the resurrection, especially given Jesus is saying this after he has been raised from the dead. Despite the protests of many Old Testament scholars, both Jesus and Paul invite their readers to be sensitively attuned to precursors, promises, and prophecies of resurrection in the Old Testament—the resurrection is subtly present in the Old Testament.

The argument of this book is not that there is a fully-fledged doctrine of the resurrection in the Old Testament. This, however, is not to say that it is absent. As a student of the Old Testament, I think the assertion that it presents a fully-fledged doctrine of the resurrection would be a difficult argument to sustain. Rather, my aim is more modest. I want to suggest that the resurrection is present in the Old Testament by way of sophisticated subtleties. Like the great jokes in *The Simpsons*, the references or allusions to the resurrection are rarely the main point of the scene. Equally, however, they are present, and for those with eyes to see they enrich the experience. Once they are observed, they are difficult to forget. This is the power of the subtle.

There are five elements to the argument in this book. The first element is the fact that God is able to raise the dead. God's power is the bedrock of any assertion about the resurrection. If God is not the all-powerful One then discussion of the resurrection is pointless. Happily, the might of the One True God is something the Old Testament establishes comprehensively. Chapter 1 will survey the account of creation and other Old Testament references to the power of God's word. The second element is Old Testament examples of God's power, explicitly over death. Chapter 2 will therefore document those occasions in the Old Testament in which the dead are brought to life. While these instances are of course of a different order from resurrection—we might call them resuscitations—they are clearly predicated on God's power over death. The third element focuses on more questionable passages in the Old Testament concerning life after death. Although not clear-cut, these are, in my judgment, highly suggestive. Chapter 3 will thus explore David's statement about following his late infant son to (or beyond?) the grave (2 Sam 12:23) and Job's confidence of being in the flesh when he sees God on the final day of human history (Job 19:25–27). The fourth element to the argument will be references to life after death in the book of Psalms. It is true that the Bible reader must be careful whenever it comes to reading biblical poetry—we are prone to reading things into poetic imagery that may not be there. Despite this, the New Testament picks up on a number of psalms and connects them explicitly to the resurrection. The use of Psalm 16:10 in the book of Acts is particularly intriguing. Hence chapter 4 will explore passages in the book of Psalms. The final element will pick up on perhaps the least subtle resurrection notes in the Old Testament: prophecies. Isaiah 25–27, Ezek 37, Hos 6 and 13, and Dan 12 all contain prophecies of life that appear to point to resurrection. In chapter 5 we will delve into these passages and consider them in light of all that has gone before.

I am convinced that Jesus was raised *according to the Scriptures*. In part this conviction is based on my view of Scripture. I believe the Bible to be divinely inspired and totally inerrant. It is therefore not hard to believe that Paul is correct in his assertion. Equally, this conviction is based on my reading of the Old Testament. I see in the Old Testament Scriptures precursors, promises, and prophecies of resurrection. There is power in its sophisticated subtleties. Perhaps you will permit me to try to convince you. My invitation to the reader is to join me in exploring the subtle pointers to the resurrection in the Old Testament to see if we can be encouraged by the way that God prepares his people to witness the remarkable event we celebrate at Easter: the resurrection of Jesus. Let me show you that Jesus really was raised according to the Scriptures and that Easter is very much present in the Old Testament.

Chapter One

Resurrection Power
The Author of Life

A Show of Strength

REREAD THE SUBTITLE IMMEDIATELY above this sentence. Unless you live (or have lived) in Northern Ireland I am certain you are not picturing what I can see in my mind's eye. That is because it is a memory from my personal childhood.

Even though it was the height of the summer, it was almost pitch black. The time was approaching midnight. A couple of hundred people loitered on a large, open green area, near a housing estate, surrounding a well-organized, large pile of wooden pallets. Soon the pile of wood was set alight. There is something mesmerizing about watching a fire take hold of a large structure in the dark. As the flames licked the black sky there was suddenly a commotion among the onlooking crowd. Four or five individuals, who I presumed to be men, dressed from head to foot in black (including balaclavas) paraded towards the middle of the green and the now towering inferno. They abruptly halted, raised their arms into the darkness above their heads, and fired their weapons a number of times towards the smoky sky.

In Northern Ireland this is known as a show of strength. It often takes place at the 11th July bonfires on the eve of the Orangemen parades commemorating King William of Orange's victory over King James II at the Battle of the Boyne. If you know anything about Irish or Northern Irish history you will appreciate how politically charged such a moment is. Unsurprisingly, this is the moment most often chosen by loyalist paramilitaries to execute a show of strength. The paramilitaries use it to prove that they are still dangerous. Its purpose is to show that they still have strength.

As intimidating as that experience was for a child, it is nothing in comparison to the show of strength at the beginning of the Bible. There we read of an astonishing show of strength:

> God says, "Let there be light." And there is (Gen 1:3).
>
> God says, "Let there be an expanse." And it is so (Gen 1:6–7).
>
> God says, "Let the waters under the heavens be gathered together." And they are (Gen 1:9).
>
> God says, "Let the earth sprout vegetation." And it does (Gen 1:11).
>
> God says, "Let there be lights in the expanse." And there are (Gen 1:14–15).
>
> God says, "Let the waters swarm with swarms of living creatures." And they do (Gen 1:20).
>
> God says, "Let the earth bring forth living creatures." And it does (Gen 1:24).
>
> God says, "Let us make man." And he does (Gen 1:26–27).

This is a remarkable show of strength—a mere voice forms everything out of nothing. God's strength is evident in that he is the author of life.

Creation and Power

Many ancient cultures passed on mythical accounts about the creation of the world, often called creation epics. These legends would have contributed to both educational and entertainment aspects of life. As families, villages, and people groups gathered in houses, around fires, and in lecture halls listeners would be enthralled with the storyteller's narrative of how the world came to be. Although the various cultures would recount different epics, they all possess a common feature: the deities/gods of that particular culture entered into conflict with someone or something evil. The ensuing divine victory is always what gave birth to the cosmos.

The Bible, originating in the midst of these alternative creation accounts, tells a very different story. According to Gen 1, before there was anything there was God. No rationalization is given. No defense is offered. No evidence is provided. There is a simple statement of fact: "In the beginning, God created . . ." (Gen 1:1). This God entered into no conflict. Quite the opposite. Out of nothing the God of the Bible brings forth everything. He fills everything. He puts everything into order. And at the end of it all he declares that it is very good (Gen 1:31). There is no chaotic clash of competitors. God speaks and everything obediently comes into existence.

In an attempt to reinforce to the children in my church the immense power necessary to create everything out of nothing by the mere use of a voice I conducted a public experiment during a Sunday service. Two children volunteered to come to the front of the building during the service. I asked them to sit at opposite ends of a small table. To one child I gave a tub of Play-Doh. To the other child I gave nothing. I then asked both of them to make a person. The child to whom I had given the Play-Doh immediately pulled it out of the tub and began rolling it to form limbs, a body, a head, and started sticking them together. The other child looked at me blankly. I asked him if he wanted help. Yes was the reply. So I suggested that he try speaking it in to existence. To be fair to him he gave it a really good go, but to no avail. Telling this story allows me publicly to thank him—Charlie—for being such a good sport. It also highlights the weakness of our words.

The image burned on everyone's mind that day was of a helpless child declaring with gusto, "Let there be a person" with no effect whatsoever. I know you will want to, so go ahead and try it yourself. Or better still, as Mr. Burns from *The Simpsons* does, go to the seaside and command the waves to cease. As either of these will demonstrate, our voices are pitifully weak. It is absolute futility to attempt to speak something into existence. Yet, this is exactly what the God of the Bible did at the beginning of time.

The significance of this to Paul's assertion that Jesus was raised according to the Scriptures should not be lost on us. Resurrection is directly related to God's ability to author life. This is the foundation upon which the remainder of this book rests—God's creative power is a key element in his ability to raise people from the dead. If God can speak everything into existence out of nothing, then surely he can bring someone back from the dead. In fact, there is a more specific episode in the creation account that further underscores this point.

Speaking Life into the Dust

Genesis 1 provides an overview summary of creation. Although it does slow down to linger over the creation of humanity (Gen 1:26–30), Gen 2 is the point at which we are given a much closer look at this episode in creation.

Those of us who are familiar with our Bibles would do well to read Gen 2 aloud to someone who has never heard it before. The wonder, bemusement, or amusement on their face will quickly remind us of how peculiar the claims of this passage (and indeed the Bible altogether) really are. Try to read this as if it was for the first time: the LORD God formed a man of dust from the ground; into the body God formed he breathed the breath of life, and the man became a living being (Gen 2:7). From the dirt you can see in your flower bed, and which God spoke into existence in the first instance, God forms a body. Into this lifeless body God then breathes—gives life—and the body becomes a living creature. This is astonishing. But God has not yet finished.

The LORD God then proceeds to remove a rib out of the man, and from this rib form another living creature (Gen 2:21–22). This living creature is named woman by the first living creature, man. Once more, out of something he has already made God forms something new. He creates another living creature—distinct from the other, yet equal and complementary.

It is important to note that these are not merely playthings that God has created. The first man and woman, Adam and Eve as they came to be known, were not the prototype Ken and Barbie. Their purpose was not merely to adorn the creation. God did not design them to be lifeless figures that he placed in a series of scenarios. Adam and Eve were not created for God's amusement. They were relational beings to whom God spoke and with whom God walked. They were also relational beings with one another. While no other creature was a fitting companion for Adam, once he saw Eve he burst out in song: At last, my companion! Not only are these living creatures relational, they are embodied. God does not create merely spirits or souls—he places the spirit/soul in a physical body, and together these constitute a whole. Sadly, because of the tragic events recorded in Gen 3, these bodies are afflicted with the disease of death. The fact that God saw fit to crown his creation with these embodied souls known as Adam and Eve reminds us that the body is important. It was created and existed before the fall—when all was very good. That is to say it is not to be escaped, but redeemed; it is not to be left dead, but raised alive. If God created these bodies, he can resurrect—recreate—them.

Living or Dying by the Word

The power of God and his word, evident in the creation account, crops up elsewhere in Scripture. There are two songs in particular in which this reality is pressed home in praise of the God who is the author of life. It would appear that God was the first to recognize and utilize the power of song.

The climax of the Song of Moses in Deut 32 draws attention to the unique status that the God of Israel possesses (vv. 39–42). He alone is God. There is no other beside him. We have already noted the uniqueness of God in the Bible's creation narrative. Unlike other so-called gods, he does not need to wrestle creation into existence out of the darkness or the grip of evil. He simply speaks. He authors life with his voice. In Deut 32 we witness something similar. As Moses, under the inspiration of the Spirit, sings, he sings God's declaration of his exclusivity, his peerlessness. A key evidence for this claim is God's ability to kill and make alive, to wound and heal. God's power over life and death are key facets in demonstrating his unequaled status. Again, the relevance for any discussion on the resurrection should be apparent. God has the ability to speak life. By God's word alone we either live or die.

In Hannah's song in 1 Sam 2:6, the imagery employed is tantalizingly suggestive of resurrection. She says that "the LORD kills and brings to life; / he brings down to Sheol and raises up." The construction of Hebrew poetry pairs the terms "kill" with "Sheol" and "life" with "raises up." That is to say God kills and sends to the grave, but he also gives life and raises up. Admittedly this is not a fully-fledged doctrine of the resurrection, but it certainly legitimizes the claim that God has power over life and death. It is at least feasible, then, to argue that God *could* raise someone from the dead. At the very least he exerts power over life and death. By God's word we either live or die.

Moses and Hannah are not alone in their ascribing to God the power to kill and make alive. In 2 Kgs 5:7 the king of Israel exclaims: "Am I God, to kill and make alive?" Although this king is not named, the quality of Israelite kings by 2 Kings is not good. They are rarely godly. Even so, this one knows enough to remember that the God of Israel, not the king of Israel, has power over life and death.

The Greatness of His Power

If you have made it this far you might feel short-changed. Yes, God created everything from nothing. Yes, God made humanity from the dust. Yes, life and death are under God's sway. But you might point out, none of that is directly related to the resurrection.

It is here that I will politely disagree with you.

I cannot prove it definitively. What exactly the apostle Paul was thinking is virtually impossible to discern. But the words he chose to write give all kinds of indications and allusions to what may have informed them. I want to suggest that some of the background I have outlined above informed some of the thoughts and phraseology that Paul used in his first prayer in Ephesians.

As Paul prays for the Ephesian church he asks God that they might experience the immeasurable greatness of his power, the working of God's great might, that was on display when he raised Jesus from the dead (Eph 1:19–20). If Jesus is raised according to the Scriptures, and this resurrection demonstrates the greatness of God's power, it could legitimately be argued that demonstrations of God's power (especially over life and death) may justifiably be considered an Old Testament precursor to the resurrection. If the resurrection of Jesus was a clear demonstration of God's power, perhaps all demonstrations of God's power that occurred prior to Jesus's resurrection in some way anticipate that resurrection. After all, if God is not the all-powerful One, discussion of the resurrection is altogether pointless. He must be able if it is to be possible. Happily, God's show of strength in the Old Testament affirms that God is indeed the author of life.

Do not take my word for it, however. The testimony of the book of Hebrews is that the great patriarch of Israel, Abraham, considered God able to raise his son Isaac from the dead (11:19). This is of course a reference to Gen 22 and the traumatic command of God to Abraham to sacrifice his only son. Depending on our mood the scene is either gut-wrenchingly sad or smirk-triggeringly humorous. Abraham and Isaac leave behind servants and transport—just the two of them head farther on. They have everything they need for the sacrifice, except the sacrifice. Either our eyes fill with tears and our gut churns with revulsion as we come to terms with what Abraham has committed to—tying his son up, laying him on the kindling, and raising the knife to slaughter the sacrifice—or our lips twitch with a smirk and our shoulders bounce with laughter as we imagine Isaac eyeing up his father on the way back to the servants and transport after the LORD provided an alternative sacrifice. Isaac's scowl would undoubtedly have been piercing, especially if he was a teenager at the time.

According to Hebrews Abraham had not lost the plot. Indeed, Gen 22 gives the clear impression that Abraham passed the test that God was making him undertake. Abraham simply trusted God. And from what Abraham knew of God he considered him able to raise Isaac from the dead. Abraham's comprehension of who God is could not have been based on much more than what we have outlined in this chapter thus far: God is the author of life. In authoring all life he has demonstrated the greatness of his power. A greatness of power which, as Paul reminds us, was exerted when Jesus was raised from the dead.

Abraham received his son back from the dead only figuratively. There are others in the Old Testament who received loved ones back from the dead more literally. It is to their stories we turn next.

Chapter Two

Resurrection Precursors
His Heart Beats

Feeling the Weight

DEATH IS DEVASTATING. THOSE of us who have sat beside a hospital bed as its occupant ceases to breathe in the silence of the night know this. Those of us who have stood in a funeral home peering into an open casket in the stillness know this. Those of us who have braced ourselves against the howling wind and driving rain as a coffin is lowered into the freezing ground know this. Those of us who in the midst of ordinary life turn to talk to someone who is no longer there know this. Death is devastating.

I recall my great-grandfather's funeral. I was a teenager when he passed away. My memory is packed full of mental images of family members with reddened eyes that were swollen with tiredness and damp cheeks that were well-watered with tears. Perhaps it is lodged in my memory because this funeral was the first one at which I served as a pallbearer—carrying the coffin for part of its journey from the church service to the grave. My great-grandfather was a farmer. He was tall and solid. As a scrawny teenager I physically felt the weight of this death. I was terrified that my bony shoulder would give out and that the heavy coffin would come crashing to the ground. Mercifully I managed.

Likewise, I recall the funeral of one of my Bible college tutors. He had taught me at undergraduate level and was supervising my postgraduate work at the time of his passing. It was about a decade after my great-grandfather's funeral. The experience this time was different. I was not family. I was not intimately involved in the funeral. I arrived at the church building shortly before the funeral service began—meeting none of the mourners—and was seated near the back of the balcony. At the end of the service, however, I felt the weight of this death. My supervisor, a man I looked up to in many ways, was gone. Despite trying to restrain myself, I broke down crying—almost uncontrollably.

I loved my supervisor no more than I loved my great-grandfather. Although I had spent hours in class and discussion with my supervisor, and we regularly exchanged emails, as a child I had spent whole days with my great-grandfather on his farm during the summer months over a number of years. The different external emotional response was simply a result of my maturing. I had grown to recognize the finality of death. I had learned that death was not natural. It was never God's intention. I was now rightly and biblically feeling the weight of death. Death is devastating.

We must feel this weight before we can appropriately appreciate the joy and wonder that accompanies the resuscitations we read of in Scripture. Feeling the weight of death helps us comprehend the goodness of our God in granting life. In the last chapter we observed the power of God and noted that this points to God's ability to resurrect the dead. In this chapter we witness him actually bringing the dead back to life.

Before proceeding there is one important note to register. I use the term resuscitation for what takes place in the following narratives because the dead are brought back to life, not glorified and resurrected. Those raised to life in this chapter will one day die again awaiting resurrection. Resuscitation should therefore be thought of as a precursor to resurrection because resurrection is a glorious extension of resuscitation.

Flatlining in Zarephath

Like the nameless refugees the news channels sporadically show trudging across borders or the nameless survivors of horrific tragedies pictured with vacant stares as they attempt to come to terms with what they have experienced, 1 Kgs 17 introduces us to a nameless widow facing equally desperate circumstances. In this single chapter of the Bible this woman knows joy, sorrow, and joy again.

Life is emotionally charged. This reality is reflected in 1 Kgs 17. A widow, evidently struggling to make ends meet, is approached by Elijah while she is gathering sticks. Elijah requests some water—a request to which the widow surprisingly acquiesces given there is a drought. But that is not enough for Elijah. He also requests something to eat. This provokes the widow to protest. The widow and her son have nothing but a handful of flour. The firewood she is gathering is for a final fire over which she will cook their final meal, before awaiting certain death. There is nothing to spare.

Elijah, however, gives the widow some instructions to follow. With nothing to lose she apparently throws caution to the wind and follows Elijah's instructions. They work. The LORD God of Israel sustains the widow, her son, and, presumably, their bold lodger with a miraculously refilling jar of flour. Day after nervous-stomach-twisting-day the widow found her jar full of flour to feed the three of them.

On a visit to Zimbabwe I witnessed women dancing out of a church building because they had been given freely some flour, rice, and soap. Memories of their beaming smiles and exuberant joy still elicit similar emotions in me, even a decade later. I can easily picture this nameless widow in 1 Kgs 17 reacting similarly every morning as some more flour tumbled out of her jar, defying reality.

This is the goodness of the God of Israel. Just when things seem too far gone—at the very moment that life feels as if it cannot get any worse—he acts in grace to sustain his people. Thus, joy. This is a timely and necessary reminder of God's love and concern for those, whether Israelite or not, who trust him with wholehearted, genuine faith. Things, however, take a turn for the worse again. Indeed, they must do for this widow to experience God's deep grace to its fullest. This too is typical of life. Just when things begin to look up—at the very moment that life feels bearable again—tragedy strikes. Thus, sorrow.

The widow's son flatlines in Zarephath. He falls ill, so ill he dies. After the miraculous provision of food, the child it sustained dies. After staving off starvation, the son succumbs to sickness. What was the point of being granted the joy of the reality-defying jar of flour? Was its sole purpose simply to deepen the sorrow?

Faced with this lifeless lad Elijah knows exactly what to do: call out to the God of Israel. Elijah has witnessed God send a drought. In this drought Elijah has experienced firsthand God's miraculous providence of the necessary sustenance. Perhaps Elijah recalls God's unrivaled power, the same power we observed in the previous chapter in Genesis, Deuteronomy, and 1 Samuel. Whatever information is filling Elijah's head, he knows there is only one option left in these circumstances: the God of Israel. Elijah prays and the child lives. The boy's heart beats. God resuscitates the child. He brings the dead back to life.

For those of us familiar with this narrative from our Sunday school days, this story probably doesn't shock us the way it should. A widow with a set of rather difficult circumstances has lost her son. He is dead. But, he does not stay dead because God intervenes. The One whose powerful word brought everything into existence—including the flour every morning—gives this boy breath again. His heart beats.

This reversal of the flatlining in Zarephath in no way seals the case for a doctrine of resurrection in the Old Testament. It is merely an additional layer to the argument that God is able to bring the dead to life. While such an assertion was merely theoretical or figurative in the light of God's creative power—outlined in the previous chapter—it is now reality. God has indeed made the dead live! This is not an isolated event either, for God does it again.

Grief and Gladness

All that took place in 1 Kgs 17 with Elijah is recognizably mirrored in 2 Kgs 4 with Elisha. To some degree the mirroring serves to legitimize Elisha as Elijah's successor. But it is surely more. God's bringing one dead boy to life was not an exception to the rule. It was something he can do again; something he will do again; something he does do again. Like the first resuscitation, this one is also a story of grief and gladness.

Unlike Elijah, Elisha does not appear to impose himself on anyone in this scenario. Instead, a wealthy woman who saw that he frequently passed her way offers hospitality. At first it is simply food to keep Elisha going, but, along with her husband, she soon establishes a permanent guest room for Elisha. Despite this generosity there is grief.

Although nameless, like the widow in 1 Kgs 17, the woman in 2 Kgs 4 differs in one key way: she is childless. Hers is the grief of never actually having. It is a strange grief. One not seen. And, it seems, one that is compounded by hope. Elisha promises this childless woman a child. The hope is almost too much for her to bear. The age of her husband appears to suggest it is not possible. But grief turns to gladness as she and her husband conceive and bear a son.

Moments change things. Sometimes for the better, sometimes for the worse. And so too this moment in 2 Kgs 4 for the Shunammite woman. After many childless years, Elisha's promise manifests itself in the birth of a boy. That moment changed things. Another moment, however, was coming.

As the narrative progresses, the boy has obviously grown. He heads out to the fields with his father. While there he is struck down with a headache. The ill-health of the boy means he is sent back to his mother for some tender loving care. His mother cares for him and offers the necessary TLC—but to no avail. The boy dies. Gladness is torn to shreds and grief is all that remains. In that moment the Shunammite woman would surely challenge the claim that it is better to have loved and lost than never to have loved at all. No! Nothing could be worse than this gladness reverting to grief.

Grief, anger, pride, shrewdness—any of these could lie behind the grief-stricken mother's next move. She seeks out Elisha. When she finds him she challenges him: had she not told him not to raise expectations? Had she not pleaded not to be given false hope?

Elisha must act. He begins to head to the house in which the boy has been left. Like Elijah before him, Elisha only has one option: pray to the LORD. He does.

Once more we witness the power of God at work. Once more that which was dead is now alive. The boy's still heart begins to beat again. Once more God reaches into the grave and declares, "Not without my say-so." Grief is once more changed to gladness.

As with 1 Kgs 17, this event in 2 Kgs 4 is not a resurrection. It is a resuscitation. Nevertheless, bringing the dead back to life is no mean feat. We are rightly astonished when medics with all of their cutting-edge, technologically advanced equipment bring someone who was technically dead back to life in a few minutes. But here is a boy who has conceivably been lying dead for hours, and with a simple prayer to the God of heaven (and no intervention with medical technology) the boy is brought back to life. This is astonishing.

The Dominion of Death

There is one more instance in the Old Testament in which the bringing to life of a dead person is narrated. It is the very last act in Elisha's ministry. In fact, Elisha is already dead. In 2 Kgs 13 we read that Elisha had died and was buried. In due course another man dies, but (as a result of a marauding band of Moabites) instead of being afforded a normal burial the man is tossed into Elisha's grave. As soon as the dead man comes into contact with Elisha's bones he comes to life again. We are told in 2 Kgs 13:21 that he revived, stood on his feet, and (presumably) walked out of the tomb. The end of Elisha's ministry reminds us that the grave has no defense against God's power.

The end of Elijah's ministry suggests the same. Rather memorably Elijah does not die but is taken to heaven miraculously. Chariots and horses of fire separate Elijah from Elisha and a whirlwind takes Elijah to heaven. He is spared the experience of death. The end of Elijah's ministry reminds us that the grave has no hold over God.

The episodes in this chapter affirm explicitly that the dominion of death is constrained by the actions of God. Two young boys escape the grasp of the grave and a dead man springs back to his feet because God intervenes. God's prophet does not taste death because God takes him from this world another way. This pattern is repeated in the New Testament. In Luke 7:11–17 Jesus brings another dead son back to life. In Luke 8:49–56 it is Jairus's dead daughter who is brought back to life by Jesus. Perhaps most famously, John 11 recounts Jesus calling Lazarus out of the grave— he had been dead for days, but the grave still could not keep him. After Jesus's days on earth it happens again. In Acts 9:36–43 Dorcas is brought back to life by God through the prayers of Peter. And in Acts 20:7–12 Paul prays and God brings back Eutychus from the dead.

All these instances, both in the Old Testament and in the New, make one simple point: God alone dictates death's dominion. Death's dominion is beholden to God's bidding. If God wishes to deny death its victim, he does so.

For God, raising the dead is as easy as waking the sleeping. My nephews and nieces love playing "Wake Up Uncle Davy." I am sure you too have played a similar game. I pretend to sleep—summoning all my acting experience from school plays, I put on my best snore—while my nephews and nieces sneak up to wake me. I pretend to be startled by their waking me, jumping and shouting, and they burst into fits of hysterical uncontrollable childish laughter. It is hilarious—if not a bit dangerous, as boys tend to launch themselves at you and girls perfect a short sharp slap across the cheek. It is funny because it is so easy to get a reaction. For God,

15

raising the dead is no more difficult than a child startling an adult pretending to sleep.

Theory and Practice

This chapter has demonstrated in practice some of the theory outlined in chapter 1. The theory of chapter 1 was that God is powerful enough to raise the dead if he so wished. If God can create everything out of nothing, including humanity, then making the dead live cannot be all that difficult for him. The ministries of the prophets Elijah and Elisha provide the evidence that demonstrates this theory. In practice God is able to raise the dead—two women can testify that their sons were indeed dead, but the God of Israel brought them back again. Indeed, there is another family who thought that their loved one was buried and gone only to find him walk back through the door again after coming into contact with Elisha's bones. This chapter shows God putting that theory into practice.

The dead being brought back to life in the Old Testament serves as a precursor to the resurrection. God is able to raise the dead. God has raised the dead. There is no reason why it cannot happen again. That which had been dead—no heartbeat, no breath, no movement, no heat—came alive—the thud of a heartbeat, the sound of expanding lungs, the twitch of a finger or an eyelid, the heat of a living body. Paul possibly had the narratives of 1 Kgs 17, 2 Kgs 4, and 2 Kgs 13 in mind as he wrote that Jesus was raised according to the Scriptures (1 Cor 15:4).

The Old Testament, however, possesses much more than mere precursors. After all, these two resuscitations are just that—resuscitations. The Christian hope is not merely to stay alive, but to be transformed. The Christian hope is to be resurrected in a glorified body to eternal life. The resuscitations in the Old Testament provide an echo of Easter in the Old Testament—life extending beyond its natural end. This is reinforced with some subtle allusions in the Old Testament to life beyond the grave. These allusions are the focus of the next chapter.

Chapter Three

Resurrection Allusions
Confident of the Unseen

Assurance of the Thing Hoped For

THREE MONTHS. THAT IS the length of time I waited for an answer from my now wife when I first asked her to be my girlfriend. Three months.

We had been friends for some time and that friendship was blossoming into romance. Being members of the same church, serving alongside one another in ministries, and spending time socially as friends offered the perfect environment for getting to know one another. As I got to know Tracy, I came to realize that she was what I hoped for in a spouse. As a result, I put myself out there, declared my feelings, and asked if they were reciprocated.

The key to this relationship being initiated was whether the end goal was marriage. Neither of us was satisfied with just seeing how it would go—marriage had to be the destination or neither of us was getting on the train. Hence the three-month wait.

I am glad to say that we remained friendly during those three months. We saw each other regularly, continued serving alongside one another, and periodically had conversations about the future. In January 2009 I finally got my answer. Tracy was in.

With this positive response I had assurance of the thing I hoped for—married life with Tracy. But we were not there yet. We had to spend some more intentional time with each other's family. We had to continue to get to know each other. We had to go ring shopping (which is a whole other story in itself!). I had to plan a proposal. We had to plan a wedding. And to top it all off, I hoped to be starting Bible college only a few months after we were married. We had assurance of the thing for which we hoped—married life together—but we were not there yet.

We were confident of that which was yet unseen.

All of this helped no end when I was plucking up the courage for the proposal—I was at least 90 percent sure my question would get a "yes" in response.

This snapshot of our romance serves as an analogy for the few passages that will be our focus in this chapter. In these passages we see individuals who are confident of the unseen. They record what we might call resurrection allusions. The previous two chapters discussed the resurrection power evidenced in God's creative activity, and subsequently looked at some resurrection precursors in the form of resuscitations. We now take another step in our exploration of what the Old Testament has to say about resurrection, and as we do we discover some resurrection allusions. King David, Job, and Jonah all demonstrate an assurance of things hoped for, a confidence in things yet unseen.

A Hint of Something More

Standing before a class of pastors-in-training, I shared about my hope of writing this book. Whenever I asked them for suggestions of passages that I might need to deal with, 2 Sam 12:23 inevitably came up. In fact, it was the first one mentioned. This did not surprise me. David's declaration "I shall go to him, but he will not return to me" in 2 Sam 12:23 is perhaps the best-known allusion to some kind of resurrection hope in the Old Testament. Having anticipated this answer from my class I pushed back gently: In what way does this point to resurrection? That question was not answered so quickly.

The narrative of 2 Sam 12 is memorable, and this statement of David's in verse 23 certainly contains hope. It is therefore understandable that we latch on to it as offering hope beyond the grave. The difficulty comes whenever we are forced to explain the way in which it offers or sustains that hope. I think we find this difficult because resurrection hope is not actually the point of this passage.

The primary point of 2 Sam 11–12 is that no one is beyond God's judgment of sin—not even God's anointed king. Further, flagrant sin brings consequences. Drastic consequences. As the prophet Nathan makes clear to King David, the child's death is a direct consequence of David's sin. The child is a result of the affair David engaged in with Bathsheba. This sin is not without consequences and judgment. Even though this is the main point of the passage, it sets up a most unusual scenario in the minds of the royal household's servants—a scenario that hints at something more: a resurrection allusion.

While the child lies ill, David mourns, fasts, and prays, but once the child dies David washes, dresses, and feasts. "What is this all about?" ask the servants (12:21). David responds with the confident assertion, "I shall go to my child" (12:23).

Most Old Testament scholars, especially those who deny the presence of resurrection hope, argue that David is merely acknowledging his own mortality. He too, like his son, will one day die. It is undeniable that he does mean this. There is no other way for him to go to his son than likewise to pass through the valley of death. But is that all he means?

I am convinced that he means something more. Do not misunderstand me, this is not a full-blown expression of Christian resurrection hope. But the statement does imply an awareness, perhaps even expectation, of an afterlife. There is a hint of something more beyond the grave. There is a personal touch to the phrase—David will go to his child. It is not merely the same location to which David is headed—the grave—it is to a person, his son, that David goes. There is a hint of something more here.

Additionally, interpreting this verse within the parameters of the entire Bible we see David's confidence in that which is yet unseen.

The fullness of David's knowledge of the afterlife will be fleshed out in the next chapter when we turn to the Psalms. Suffice to say at this point that he knows there is more to come (see Pss 16:10; 17:15). All that is recorded for us in 2 Samuel is that David is confident of going to his son. This verse therefore alludes to something more. It suggests a confidence even in the absence of complete knowledge.

It is like switching on your car ignition. If, like me, you have little awareness or understanding of all the moving parts inside the engine, each morning you have confidence in the absence of complete knowledge—you trust that as you turn the key, the engine will start. This is confidence in the absence of complete knowledge. So too with David. He may not have been able to outline in detail what would happen beyond the grave or how exactly it would happen, but, it seems, he was confident that death was not the end. There is something more. King David's declaration in 2 Sam 12:23 hints at it.

This should be a great encouragement to us. For, although we have the fullness of God's revelation in his Son and through his Scriptures, there is much that remains a mystery to us. There are many questions to which we have no satisfactory answer and will have no satisfactory answer this side of the grave. Not a few of these unanswered questions concern lost loved ones and our experience beyond the grave, in heaven, and, ultimately, in the new heavens and the new earth. But if David, at his point in redemptive history, can have assurance of things hoped for, and confidence in that which is yet unseen, how much more can we?

David merely hinted at something more. What we see in Job is much more than a hint, however.

Overconfident?

By nature or nurture, I am skeptical. Perhaps this is due to difficult experiences in my childhood, but equally I may just be a naturally untrusting person. At its worst my skepticism is sinfully thinking the worst of people. At its best my skepticism is exercising the gift of discernment. In the end, my propensity to be skeptical means I distrust people who are overly confident—particularly people who have something to say about everything.

I am certain that you too will have met people like this. It does not matter whether it is space travel or customer service, ancient Egypt or the latest gadget, medical conditions or celebrities, they have experienced it, know all there is to know about it, and can put you straight as to what you need to know about it. People who have something to say about everything make me clam up. I do not trust them. I am skeptical that any one person can possibly have so much to say about so many different issues—and say it all with such confidence.

This makes me wonder if I might have been skeptical with Job had I met him. Just look at what he has to say in Job 19:

> For I know that my Redeemer lives,
>   and at the last he will stand upon the earth.
> After my skin has been thus destroyed,
>   yet in my flesh I will see God,
> Whom I shall see for myself,
>   and my eyes shall behold and not another. (vv. 25–27)

These verses are dripping with confidence about something Job cannot know—can he?

As we have already noted, lots of people will say that Job can have no knowledge of what is to come. Life beyond the grave and resurrection hope are alien concepts to Old Testament saints, it is claimed. This climactic statement in Job is therefore debated. So, is Job overconfident? Is he speaking out of blind ignorance? Is this mere speculation on his account? For a number of reasons I believe the answer to these questions is no.

Job is not an individual who claims to have something to say about everything. He does not claim to be an expert in everything. In fact, at times he is lost for words. After experiencing horrific grief at unbearable events he spends a whole week in silence with his so-called friends (Job 2:13). Then, near the end of the entire experience God speaks to Job and Job confesses that he has no answer (40:3–5). Throughout the book Job asserts his innocence, wrestles with his sufferings, and acknowledges that he is all out of answers. This humility is striking and makes comments like those in Job 19:25–27 stand in stark contrast to the rest of the book.

Consider that Job has lost his home, his children, his livelihood, and his health. On any balance of probability this would be evidence against Job's deity—either his God cannot be real, or else he is powerless. But this is not how Job sees it. He remains confident that his Redeemer lives. Despite the apparent evidence before his tear-stung eyes, Job knows his God lives. There is more: Job is equally certain that this God, in the end, will stand on the earth. He will come to Job's rescue. Job will be justified. This is Job's confidence: God, his Redeemer, not only lives but will come to fight his cause. There is a day coming when Job will be declared innocent.

Confidence of Job's vindication is then followed by confidence of his demise. Job is confident of his death. In moving from verse 25 to 26 in our Bibles we move from the triumph of an innocent verdict to the reality of a designated grave. Job knows he will die. His skin will be destroyed; it will decompose, rot, fade away. This must not be lost on us. Job fully comprehends that he goes the way of everyone else, including his children. There is no privileged escape for him. But much like David, Job is confident that the grave is not the end. More is to come.

Job is not only sure of vindication and death, but also of seeing God. The certainty is that Job will see God after his death. More remarkable is the claim that Job, whose skin has been destroyed, will once more be clothed in his flesh for his meeting with God. Without getting too technical it must be admitted that the Hebrew behind our translation is notoriously difficult to translate. Some scholars therefore suggest that the translation should be *without* flesh, not *in* flesh. A footnote in your Bible translation might indicate this. However, given that Job says he will see God with his own eyes in verse 27, which were presumably destroyed with the rest of his flesh in verse 26, I find it difficult to ignore the implication that

Job is confident of new flesh on the far side of the grave in which he will see God face to face. It is a scandalously bold claim.

This small passage in Job is astonishing! It is most certainly a resurrection allusion. After being destroyed by death Job is confident of being reclothed in his flesh in order to see God. Note two features of this assertion.

First, Job's confidence should strike the reader given the circumstances in which he finds himself. There is no hint of doubt in this declaration. Absolute certainty characterizes Job's comments. His God lives, his death will come, his flesh will be remade, and his God will meet and vindicate him. Just as David was certain of meeting his son on the far side of the grave, so Job is certain of meeting his God on the far side of the grave.

Second, Job's language should strike the reader. The destruction of flesh, the seeing God with his own eyes, the being enfleshed again all stand out. They are simply staggering claims, especially if we date Job with many scholars in the same time period as Genesis. Job is describing exactly what Paul describes in 1 Cor 15—the sowing of the old body and the reaping of the new. This is resurrection.

If Job's comments stood alone in the Old Testament we might justifiably be nervous about placing such weight on them. We might fear that we are making a mountain out of a molehill. But on the basis of resurrection power and precursors, observed in the previous two chapters, it is almost impossible to read Job's words any other way.

As we work our way through the Christian canon, we are beginning to build up a more detailed picture of Easter in the Old Testament. This passage in Job adds a significant amount of detail in one go, especially concerning our being re-fleshed on the other side of the grave. There is great comfort here for those of us who have suffered tragically in this life. No matter the pain, no matter the hurtful counsel, no matter the consistent passing of time towards our unavoidable end, something better awaits us beyond the grave. Our Redeemer lives. At the last, in the end, he will stand on earth and vindicate those who by grace alone have placed their faith alone in Christ alone. And although we may have had our skin destroyed long before this happens, we will be enfleshed once more. In that new flesh we will see God with our own eyes.

Is Job overconfident? Not according to the events that transpired three days after Jesus's death.

The Resurrection of Jonah

Make sure you read that heading correctly. Not the resurrection of Jesus, but the resurrection of Jonah. The resurrection allusions connected to King David and Job prompt me to see Jonah in a different light. Jonah's is most likely a figurative resurrection—although some contend that it may well be literal—but it alludes to another.

The book of Jonah is famous for reasons other than resurrection. The great fish is what looms large in most people's minds when Jonah is mentioned. It is in the psalm that Jonah utters from the gut of the great fish that resurrection hope is found, however. In this psalm, or, perhaps better, prayer, recorded in Jonah 2, Jonah is figuratively portrayed as dead on the seafloor (vv. 5–6b). He is as good as dead. The downward journey that Jonah has been on for two chapters has hit rock bottom.

But God. God intervenes: "Yet you brought up my life from the pit, O LORD my God" (v. 6c). God has transformed death into life. Jonah is on his way up from the watery grave. Surely, some might say, this is simply Jonah praising God for rescuing him from the great fish. It has nothing to do with resurrection, does it? That might be a fair point if it were not for the fact that Jonah utters these words of praise from the gut of the great fish. In the pitch black, with great fish bile sloshing around his feet, Jonah is certain of life. It is remarkable. Only after this psalm is prayed does Jonah find himself on dry land (2:10). In Jonah's psalm we are once again witnessing an assurance of things hoped for and confidence in that which is yet unseen.

This reading of Jonah finds further support by noting that Jonah is in his "grave" for three days (1:17) and recalling that Jesus himself pointed to Jonah as a sign of his impending resurrection

(Matt 12:38–42) Indeed, in this Jesus is likewise expressing assurance of things hoped for, confidence in that which is yet unseen.

If this is the confidence that Old Testament saints like David, Job, and Jonah possessed, how much more we who have the record of Jesus's resurrection and the promise that he was the first among many to rise (Rom 8:29; Col 1:18). Although we still do not see the hope that lies beyond the grave with perfect clarity, we do see it more clearly than the saints of old did. If David, Job, and Jonah viewed resurrection hope through the thick early morning fog, we now view it through the dissipating mid-morning mist.

Piecing Together the Puzzle

It might be helpful at this point to consider our exploration of the Old Testament, initiated by Paul's phrase "raised according to the Scriptures," as piecing together a puzzle. At this stage we might consider ourselves to have the border in place. We have found all the corner pieces and the flat-edged pieces and put them all together. We now have a frame within which all the other pieces fit.

This frame reveals to us that God possesses resurrection power. This power, while demonstrated in creation, is evident in resurrection precursors—dead individuals who were brought back to life. On this basis it seems that other, arguably more debatable, comments might legitimately be understood as resurrection allusions. We will continue to add detail as we turn to explore the Psalms, or what we might call resurrection poems.

Chapter Four

Resurrection Poems
Delivered from Death

The Bible's Abstract

VIRTUALLY EVERY ACADEMIC JOURNAL article carries at its beginning an abstract. An abstract is a short, two-hundred-word paragraph that outlines the argument of the article. They are hugely helpful as they frequently save time. Instead of wasting hours reading articles that are not relevant or move in an unexpected direction, an abstract's one paragraph summary that can be read in sixty seconds describes what is contained in the article. All the key elements that a reader wants to know about any given article can be found in the abstract—it is a distillation of the main points.

The Psalter is the Bible's abstract. Martin Luther, the Reformer, has long been credited with calling the Psalter the Bible in miniature. The label is accurate. Everything we find elsewhere in the Bible is reflected to a greater or lesser degree in the Psalter. Creation is echoed in many psalms. Historical psalms recount poetically the exodus from Egypt, Sinai experience, and wilderness wanderings. There are royal psalms connected to the king, particularly the Davidic king. Exuberant joy and deepest sorrow are reflected in the emotion of the psalms. Other psalms anticipate the rebuilding of Jerusalem and the return of exiles. Some point forward to a messianic figure who is later revealed as Jesus Christ. Reading the Psalms from beginning to end outlines the whole of Scripture's story line. The Psalter is the Bible's abstract.

It should therefore be unsurprising to find references to the resurrection in the Psalter. If all that is present in the rest of the Bible is in some way reflected in the Psalter, then surely the resurrection, which is so prominent in the New Testament, should likewise make an appearance. Indeed, as we have been observing, resurrection hope is present in the Old Testament and Christ has truly been raised according to the Scriptures—resurrection hope should therefore be present in the Psalter.

It is.

There is clear evidence throughout the Psalter that death is not the end. More lies beyond the grave, according to the psalmists. What we therefore read in the Psalter are resurrection poems. There are repeated refrains of deliverance from death, life beyond the grave, living in the presence of God, and the electrifying truth that God will not let his chosen people see corruption in the grave. The Bible's abstract carries these notes of resurrection in its poems.

Delivered from Death

The world of cosmetics—be they ointments for external beauty, medication for internal health, or surgery to reverse the irrepressible effects of aging—is attempting to answer a question asked in the Psalter: "What man can live and never see death?" (Ps 89:48). The cosmetic world cries out, "He who uses the latest anti-aging cream," "She who consumes the correct balance of multivitamins," "Anyone brave and rich enough to embark on surgery." Psalm 89, in a parallel line rephrases the question: "Who can deliver his soul from the power of Sheol?" (v. 48)—Sheol being the place of the dead. Again, the cosmetic world responds, "The scientists, the doctors, the health care professionals." The rhetorical questions of Psalm 89 scoff at the pitiful answers offered up by modern medicine. No one can halt the evidence of age for long. The conveyor belt that inexorably inches us towards our death has no emergency stop. But as we have witnessed elsewhere in the Old Testament, Scripture's testimony is clear: death is not the final destination.

The answer to the questions posed in Psalm 89 are found elsewhere in the Psalter. Spoiler alert! The answer is God.

The Psalter's doctrine of God is rich. Its presentation of him is multifaceted. But perhaps the overarching category is that of God as Savior/Redeemer. Of course, this in turn is a rich and comprehensive concept in the Psalter, speaking of much more than simply conversion. Redemption is experienced physically, emotionally, spiritually, mentally, and in various other ways throughout the Psalter. David rightly declares in Psalm 68:20, "Our God is a God of salvation." He proceeds to explain that this salvation extends to deliverances from death (v. 20). In the context of Ps 68 it appears that this means God has granted victory in war. Death did not devour David on this occasion. God saved David from death.

The concept of deliverance from death is escalated in other psalms. In Ps 86:13 God demonstrates his steadfast love by delivering David from the depths of Sheol. As noted above, Sheol is the place of the dead—it is from there that David's soul has been delivered. A similar sentiment is echoed in Ps 116:8: "For you have delivered my soul from death." Intriguingly, both references refer to the psalmist's soul. The use of this term in the Old Testament is not an attempt to differentiate between the external and the internal, or the material and the spiritual. It is rather a reference to the entire person, the very essence of who any individual is. The whole person is delivered from the domain of the dead. This is David's testimony. This is the psalmists' testimony.

While these references are referring to God's snatching the psalmist away from death, as an adult might snatch a child out of the way of oncoming traffic, Ps 49:15 portrays the same idea much more provocatively. There the sons of Korah confess that God ransoms souls from the power of Sheol. Indeed, it is more personal: "God will ransom my soul from the power of Sheol, for he will receive me." The image conveyed here is of God's buying someone back from the dead for himself—the child has been struck by the traffic, and lies lifeless on the road, but his life can be rescued.

Reading the verse in this way is supported by noting a similarity between the Hebrew wording at the end of Ps 49:15 and that of Gen 5:24 and 2 Kgs 2:3, 5, 9. In those passages Enoch and Elijah, respectively, are taken to be with God—he receives them. They escape death because God delivers them from it. So too in Ps 49, God receives those he ransoms from Sheol, those he delivers from death. Like the claw cranes in arcades in which teddy bears are picked up and removed from their glass case, so God reaches into the grave and plucks his people out of death's confinement.

These resurrection poems teach us that God delivers from death.

Made to Live

The Psalter makes it clear that deliverance from death is only the first step. It is not as if once delivered from death God abandons his people to their own devices. No. Those who are delivered from death are made to live again—or, in New Testament language, new creations.

David first alludes to this at the end of Ps 17. Beyond death David is certain of seeing God's face. He will awake to this reality. The metaphor of sleeping and awaking is frequently used to speak of the reality of resurrection. That is what is happening at the end of Ps 17. David is evidently facing great hardship, which in part seems to be God's testing him. His enemies surround him seeking to throw him to the ground (v. 11). This intimates a desire to kill, destroy. If so, then David confesses he will awake from this death to see God and be satisfied with his post-death experience (v. 15). A further reason for seeing Ps 17 as a resurrection poem is the contrast between the men of the world, whose portion is this life in verse 14, and David, whose hope is for when he awakes in the next (v. 15). The anticipation of awaking to see God's face is not a hope for some ethereal existence. It is the expectation of living again.

David develops this in Ps 30:3. The imagery of sleeping and waking appears again. While one might weep with the darkness, in the morning there is joy. How? God brings up souls from Sheol. We have already mentioned both souls and Sheol above, but the parallel line in Ps 30:3 elaborates exactly what David means: "You restored me to life from those who go down to the pit." In other words, David is being made to live again. Sheol and the pit are places of death and despair. But from these very places David is confident of life and joy.

While we must be careful that we do not force poetic language to say more than it is saying, this verse is provocative. It is not suggesting merely that God has delivered David from death. It goes further. The implication is that David was in Sheol, in the pit. It was from that very place that God had brought him up and restored him to life. It is the difference between intercepting your child on the way to the bin with your car keys—thus delivering the keys from the bin—and being forced to dig through the bin to bring out the keys already deposited there. God has stretched into the pit, brought David out, and made him to live again.

Psalm 71, although anonymous, echoes the same idea as David's psalms 17 and 30. In Ps 71:20 the elderly author of the psalm (note the grey hairs in v. 18) states that God will revive him. From the depths of the earth, God will bring him up again. The imagery here is just as striking as that which has gone before. Indeed, the increase of greatness (v. 21) and the jubilant praise (vv. 22–24) highlight the magnitude of what the psalmist expects God to do for him.

In these three psalms—17, 30, 71—the authors clearly expect to be made to live after experiencing Sheol, the pit, or the depths of the earth. This is no easy believism. It is necessary to experience the pain of death, but after that there is life. We talk about scarifying our lawns. This process requires killing the moss in the lawn, often turning it black. Instead of green grass there are large patches of dying moss scarring the lawn. This is followed by vigorously raking, either manually or by machine, to remove the dead moss. After that the lawn looks black and bald. But within a few weeks new grass soon grows. The lawn becomes thicker and lusher. The green of the grass is more vibrant. The lawn is made to live again. So too with these resurrection poems. Their authors must experience the blackness of death before the delight of being made to live again.

In the Presence of God

Whose presence do you crave? Your spouse's? A dear and trusted friend's? A sports star's? A musician's? A celebrity's? The president's? The king's? All of us have a list of people whose presence we crave; people whose presence we enjoy; and people whose presence we benefit from. Satisfaction, ecstasy, and profit are all found in God's presence. After being delivered from death and being made to live again, the psalmists tell us that this new life is lived in the presence of God.

This new life experienced by the psalmists is lived in the presence of God.

There is a subtle allusion to this in Ps 9:13–14. Here we read of a journey from the gates of death to the gates of daughter Zion. This personification of the city of Jerusalem amplifies the metaphor of Zion being a city of life, security, and God's presence. In other words, Zion is the place to be—it is the opposite of death. The implication of these verses is not only deliverance from death and living again, but also that this living again will take place only in the presence of God. If God's people are not in the grave, they are with their God.

More explicitly, Ps 17:15 states that the psalmist will behold God's face in righteousness. There was no FaceTime in King David's day. To behold someone's face was to be actually in their presence. In Ps 17:15, then, David is telling us that he will find himself in God's presence. This is not unlike Job's confidence, which we observed in the previous chapter. It is important to remember that here in Ps 17 the experience of God's presence is connected to the concept of awaking, which, as we have noted, is a common metaphor for resurrection. This will become even more apparent in the next chapter.

The reality of this is ratcheted up again in Ps 73:24. There Asaph confesses that God will guide him with counsel and after that receive him to glory. The psalm suggests that this counsel will lead Asaph through a tumultuous life, during which the wicked seem to prosper. The counsel Asaph receives, however, is that the wicked will not prosper in the life to come. It seems in this context that to be received into glory afterwards suggests after life. I have confidence in such a suggestion because Asaph continues to write that God in heaven is all he has and there is nothing on earth he desires—he craves God's presence (v. 25). Even though Asaph's flesh and heart will fail—death?—God will be his portion forever (v. 26). Indeed, Asaph will be near his God (v. 28). The end of Ps 73 is all about enjoying and benefiting from the presence of God. More, it seems to be that God's presence will be enjoyed in this way in eternity to come.

The Psalter's poetry points to the presence of God, in which life is lived after deliverance from death. This is why we can call them resurrection poems. With confidence we can cry with the psalmist, and Christ (see Luke 23:46), into your hands we commit our spirits (Ps 31:5). If God can deliver us from death, make us live again, and bring us into his presence, we need no longer fear death.

And yet, the Psalter has even more to say.

Imperishable

In a most astonishing declaration David is certain that God will not abandon his soul to Sheol or let his holy one see corruption (Ps 16:10). Among all the startling phrases in all the resurrection poems within the Psalter, this one immediately grasps our attention.

On one level David is simply reasserting his confidence in God's protection: a common theme in book 1 of the Psalter (Pss 1–41). But this confidence clearly reaches beyond the limits of this life. David proceeds in the very next verse to anticipate life in the presence of God forevermore (Ps 16:11). He will not perish in the pit; he will not see corruption. This can be nothing else than David's looking to the resurrection.

My confidence in this reading of Ps 16 is not misplaced. Both Peter and Paul quote this psalm when preaching about the resurrection of Jesus. These sermons are recorded for us in the book of Acts.

In Acts 2 we have a record of Peter's speech on the day of Pentecost. Peter points to David speaking of bodily hope beyond the grave, quotes Ps 16, and then takes three steps with the psalm. First, Peter argues that David died, was buried, and that his grave can be seen by those in Jerusalem (v. 29). Second, David was known to have prophetic capacity (2 Sam 23:1; Ps 110:1; Acts 2:30) and knew that God would place a Davidic descendant on the throne forever (2 Sam 7:1216; Ps 132:11; Acts 2:30). Third, David must then be witnessing to the resurrection, and, more specifically, the resurrection of Jesus (v. 31). Here is apostolic exegesis labeling Ps 16 as a prophetic resurrection poem. The apostle Paul makes virtually the same exegetical steps in Acts 13:35–37.

In 1 Cor 15:42–55 (but especially v. 53) Paul explains that the mortal will put on immortality and that the perishable will put on the imperishable. After reading Ps 16 this does not appear to be an original idea. Paul is simply reiterating what he has already observed in the Old Testament. These resurrection poems taught Paul that the grave is not the end.

Destination

Booking holidays always leads to false expectations. Browsing photographs of idyllic locations quickly encourages us to click the purchase button, as we can picture ourselves lying poolside in the sun, exploring fascinating city centers, or surveying breathtaking landscapes. As we click the purchase button, we are not envisaging the last-minute packing rush, the children waging war in the back of the car, the airport security line that remains static, or the questionable public transport on offer to get us through the last leg of the journey. In short, traveling is horrible, but it is worth it for the destination—usually.

The Psalter makes this very argument with its resurrection poems. As is often noted, the Psalms are real and raw. They sugarcoat nothing. Life is hard, the wicked often prevail, and coping with it all frequently prods us to the breaking point. This life, however, with its certain destination of the grave is not all there is. In fact, death and the grave are not so much the destination as part of the journey. The Psalter repeatedly testifies that the grave is not our destination. Instead, the Psalms sing to us that God delivers from death, makes the dead to live again, brings the living dead into his presence, and promises that they are now imperishable. These resurrection poems affirm that there is life beyond the grave. More detail about what that life looks like can be found in resurrection prophecies, and it is to those we now turn.

Chapter Five

Resurrection Prophecies

Raised from the Grave

The Final Few Pieces

ARE YOU EXCITED?

At the end of chapter 3 I suggested that we might consider this exploration of resurrection in the Old Testament like piecing together a puzzle. By the end of chapter 3 we had the frame in place—all the corner and edge pieces of the puzzle were arranged correctly. The picture was then filled out in our last chapter as we learned that the Psalter is full of resurrection poems. These poems teach us that God delivers from death, makes us live again, does so in his presence, and makes us imperishable. In this chapter we now piece together the final parts of the jigsaw. By the end of this chapter our view of resurrection in the Old Testament should be complete. This excites me—does it excite you?

The prophets of the Old Testament are an eclectic, eccentric bunch. Their preaching carried cutting critiques, mystifying messages, and glorious guarantees. They were at once the people's best friend and their worst enemy. But, above all, they were sent by God and communicated his word.

It is in the proclamation of this word of God delivered by the prophets that the final few pieces of the Old Testament resurrection puzzle are clicked into place. When this is done the picture is unmistakable and most compelling: Jesus's resurrection was certainly according to the Scriptures.

Resurrection as a Metaphor

I have witnessed some remarkable sights in my relatively short life. I have ascended the Atlas Mountains in Morocco, visited Victoria Falls in Zimbabwe, watched the Houses of Congress in action in Washington, DC, and munched on guinea pig in Moquegua, Peru. None of these, however, comes close to what Ezekiel witnessed in the Valley of Dry Bones—even if it was only a vision. It is here that we begin our foray into the prophetic books.

Ezekiel 37 is likely a familiar episode. Ezekiel is taken in the Spirit of the LORD and set down in a valley. The valley is full of bones, bones that had been there for a while. There was no flesh on the bones; they were dry. Listen carefully and you can almost hear them clacking against one another as they slip down the valley slope. God then asks the prophet, "Can these bones live?" (v. 3), to which the prophet wisely answers, "Only you know" (v. 3). They can! God commands Ezekiel to prophesy over the bones. When he does the bones rattle and join together, and sinews, flesh, and skin begin to clothe them (v. 8). To make these renewed bodies live the prophet is then commanded to prophesy for the breath/wind/ Spirit to come into them—and he does (v. 10). A throng of living people now populate what was once a valley of bones.

In verses 11–14 we are told the meaning of this event. Israel is the valley of dry bones—dead in exile; but at the word of God they can be resurrected—return to the land with God's blessing. Surely this then means that this passage is not about resurrection, but about Israel reclaiming the promised land. Not quite.

God is so explicit as to say in his interpretation of this vision that he will open the graves and raise his people from them (vv. 12–13). He is going to make them live again (v. 14). In the first instance these "graves" are probably the countries of exile in which the Israelites now find themselves. But given what we have seen so far in the Old Testament, I would be hesitant to say that this rules out anything more. I suggest that it could be a subtle foreshadowing of what is to come for the new Israel of God—as Paul calls the church in Gal 6:16.

Nevertheless, even if this resurrection language is simply intended to serve as a metaphor—and that alone—the concept of resurrection must have been intelligible to the people for the metaphor to be meaningful. Ezekiel must have had some category for resurrection in order to comprehend this vision. At the very least he knew after the visions what resurrection was.

Ezekiel is not alone in using resurrection as a metaphor. Hosea may not have had as remarkable a vision as Ezekiel, but he still leans on the resurrection metaphor in his prophecy. In fact, he adds a little more detail and a little more triumph. In Hos 6:2 the prophet encourages the beleaguered people with the promise that they will be raised on the third day. God's reviving of his people is resurrection. This detail of the third day should be added to Jonah's living again after three days. We can now begin to see some of the finer, more nuanced ways in which Christ was raised according to the Scriptures. He too was raised on the third day.

At the end of his prophecy, amid an oracle of judgment, Hosea once more alludes to God's defeat of death (13:14). God asks two rhetorical questions: Shall I ransom them from the power of Sheol? Shall I redeem them from death? Although the implied answer to these rhetorical questions is no—that is, as an act of judgment God should leave his people in the grave—the questions once again presuppose God's power over the grave and the concept of resurrection as intelligible to Hosea and his hearers. These questions imply that God has power to raise his people from the grave. These two rhetorical questions are followed by two questions that declare God's absolute power and victory over the grave: "O Death, where are your plagues? O Sheol, where is your sting?" (Hos 13:14). These are the questions Paul echoes in 1 Cor 15:55 to declare victory over the grave in and through Jesus Christ. It is therefore worth noting that some commentators interpret these lines not as questions but as statements of hope in Hosea.

While some may object that Ezekiel and Hosea merely employ resurrection as a metaphor, I want to press back gently and say the fact that they use it as a metaphor is telling. If their hearers had been reading the passages we have already addressed in this book, then the concept of redemption as resurrection would have made sense. Other prophets, however, are much more explicit.

Swallowing Up Death

I mentioned a trip into the Atlas Mountains while in Morocco. As magnificent and remarkable as that trip was, I was violently ill on one of the days in the mountains—I am talking about projectile. There is a picture of the group sitting around the breakfast table and I am so grey that I am almost translucent. The last thing I drank before being sick was some mint tea. It was not the tea that made me ill, I had been drinking it for days, but because it was the last taste in my mouth, my body identified it as something to be avoided. This proved problematic whenever we visited a family a couple of days later. Moroccan culture values hospitality highly and to refuse what is given is an act of great dishonor. Imagine my horror, then, as a glass of mint tea was placed in front of me. Even the scent of it was turning my stomach, never mind the thought of drinking it. What was I going to do?

Thankfully, my friend sitting beside me kindly offered to drink my tea for me. Once he had emptied his glass of mint tea, we subtly swapped glasses and he swallowed my mint tea too. It was gone and the contents of my stomach remained where they were.

My friend's action is an echo of what Isaiah says God will do to death—God will swallow up death forever.

Isaiah chapters 25–27 is perhaps the most compelling presentation of resurrection in the Old Testament. In flashes throughout these chapters the prophet promises that death has lost its sting because of the hope of resurrection. These chapters conclude the second major movement in Isaiah's mammoth book, chapters

13–27, which addresses the Holy One of Israel's relationship with the nations. In earlier chapters it is made explicitly clear that God, the Holy One of Israel, will humble and defeat enemy nations. Oracle follows oracle packed full of doom and gloom for the nations. Their defeat is total in Isa 24. The atmosphere, however, changes drastically in Isa 25.

In Isa 25:6 the prophet tells us that God will prepare a banquet for all peoples—all nations. This is good news. As is the next verse which promises the removal of the doom and gloom that was blanketed over the nations in the monotonous oracles. This is accomplished by God's swallowing death (v. 8). The revolting glass that sits before the nations is gone—God has swallowed it himself. Tears are wiped away. After the humbling defeat articulated in the previous chapters, new life is now promised in Isa 25. Hope springs eternal.

There is yet a more detailed puzzle piece to put in place from Isaiah. Not only is death swallowed up, but people will be raised from the grave. In the most explicit language employed so far, Isaiah sings a song of joy in response to God's swallowing death forever. In this song we read,

> Your dead shall live; their bodies shall rise.
> > You who dwell in the dust, awake and sing for joy!
> For your dew is a dew of light,
> > and the earth will give birth to the dead. (26:19)

It could not be clearer. The dead live. Bodies will rise. Those dead in the dust will awake and sing. The prophet then employs the graphic imagery of the earth giving birth to its dead—the grave cannot and will not hold them. Death is swallowed and so the dead will sing.

Isaiah is unmistakably assuring his readers that the grave is not the end. Although, as we have seen, there have been precursors, allusions, and poems about such resurrection, it is not until Jesus strides out of the tomb that it is clear that Isaiah was right. In Jesus's resurrection the dead are promised life, bodies rise from the grave, those in the dust awake, and the earth gives birth to her dead (Matt 27:51–53). Isaiah tells us God will swallow up death forever. Jesus shows us that God has swallowed up death forever.

The Sleeping Awake

The final prophecy to be considered in this chapter is found in Dan 12. Even though its narratives make frequent appearances in children's ministry programs, the second half of Daniel is notoriously difficult to interpret. In various places I have heard Bryan Chapell confess to beginning a sermon series in Daniel but shelving it halfway through and admitting to his congregation that he had no idea what the second half of Daniel meant![1] I do not pretend to know all that is taking place in the apocalyptic passages in Dan 7–12. There is, however, a very clear prophecy concerning resurrection in Dan 12.

The last chapter of Daniel is about the last times. Daniel himself is informed that what he has been shown and told is for the time of the end (12:4, 9). While much of it remains shrouded in mystery, at least one thing is clear: all people will be resurrected. First, let's explore the theme of resurrection and then we will address the fact that all people will be resurrected.

Daniel 12:2 could rightly be called a pivotal text in any discussion of resurrection in the Old Testament. This is because it is so clear. In our chapter on the Psalms, we have already seen how the imagery of sleeping and awaking is related to resurrection. It makes sense. Surely you too have stood beside an open coffin and heard someone say, "It looks like he is just sleeping." Death is a final type of sleep. But, like every other type of sleep, it is a sleep from which we will awake. That this is not a mere metaphor is evident in that the awakening is followed by everlasting consequences. Those who have been awoken from sleeping in the dust awake to eternal repercussions. The implication is that the resurrected are part of a

---

1. See, for example, "Preaching Through Difficult Parts of the Bible," April 2, 2014, https://www.thegospelcoalition.org/video/preaching-through-difficult-parts-of-the-bible/. After figuring it out, Bryan Chapell did return to Daniel to preach through chapters 7–12.

new world in which death will no longer exert its power. Whether the eternal consequences are pleasant or punitive does not matter, they will last. As Isaiah makes clear, death is swallowed up and the earth will one day give birth to her dead. After this happens, we are all at God's mercy.

Even though English translations of Dan 12:2 use the term "many," the Hebrew word more frequently carries connotations of all, or multitudes. It is therefore not a limited resurrection envisaged in Dan 12:2, but a general resurrection. Too often Christians talk as if only Christians will be resurrected. This is incorrect. Christians are the only ones looking forward to resurrection. The reason for this is because the righteous will be raised from the grave to everlasting life. The unrighteous, however, will be raised from the grave to everlasting contempt—an all too different experience. All people will be resurrected—some to joy, others to judgment.

These prophecies might have been some time off from Daniel's day. He too, however, is promised resurrection: "You shall rest and stand in your allotted place at the end of days" (12:13). In fact, he already experienced a metaphorical resurrection which foreshadows Jesus's and his own. Daniel 6 records Daniel's death sentence in the lion's den. This "tomb" was sealed with a stone (6:17), but in the early morning (v. 19) Daniel was raised alive (v. 23). What is foreshadowed in Dan 6 is asserted in Dan 12, realized in Jesus's resurrection, and anticipated on the last day. While the last days may be closer to our day the same promise (or warning) confronts us—we too will one day stand in our allotted place. It is quite possible that you, reader, have an interest in the Old Testament but not in the Messiah it proclaims. If that is the case, know that Jesus died and rose again in order to secure for you everlasting life rather than everlasting contempt. All you need to do, as Peter—who preached the resurrection—makes clear, is repent and believe (Acts 2:38).

As Christians this climactic prophecy, which crowns this book's exploration, solidifies our resurrection hope. Despite the necessity for Daniel to shut up these words and seal this book (12:4) in his day, when Christ burst forth from the grave these resurrection truths reverberated around the globe. What we see in Jesus's resurrection is foretold in Daniel: the sleeping will awake to sleep no more. We will be raised from the grave to reap our eternal rewards.

A Cumulative and Compelling Case?

The apostle Paul had no hesitation in asserting that Jesus was raised according to the Scriptures. It is often lost on us as New Testament Christians that what Paul is saying in 1 Cor 15:4 is that the Old Testament gave us fair warning that Jesus would be raised from the grave. I trust that if you have read this far you now have a good idea of the possible passages that Paul had in mind.

No single chapter in this book clinches the argument that resurrection is present in the Old Testament—except perhaps the present one. Together, however, resurrection power, precursors, allusions, poems, and prophecies construct a cumulative and compelling case that becomes difficult to ignore. It is plausible that Paul was thinking about Genesis, Kings, Samuel, Job, Jonah, Psalms, Ezekiel, Hosea, Isaiah, and Daniel when he asserted that Jesus was raised on the third day according to the Scriptures. It is therefore vitally important that we become ever more familiar with our Old Testament in order better to understand our New Testament.

A careful reading of the Old Testament reveals that there are subtle—but powerful, recall the introduction—hints towards resurrection sprinkled throughout. As in a garden in spring, there are lots of tiny green shoots that are hard to identify but point to life yet to come. Whether it is God's creative power, the resuscitations under the ministries of Elijah and Elisha, the precursors in Job and Jonah, or the poems that are rehearsed in the New Testament, they all testify to life beyond the grave. It is only in Jesus Christ, however, that we see them blossom in full view into resurrection from the grave—and with this, the hope that we too will one day blossom from the grave.

Jesus was indeed raised according to the Scriptures; Easter is indeed present in the Old Testament.

Conclusion

Knowing the Scriptures
and the Power of God

Learning How to Read the Scriptures

HAVE YOU NOTICED THE increasing market for books on how to read other books? For me it started with Tony Reinke's *Lit! A Christian Guide to Reading Books.* This then opened up another world of books on reading, such as Mortimer J. Adler and Charles Van Doren's *How to Read a Book: The Classic Guide to Reading.* Heeding the advice in these books I began to read classic fiction instead of my heretofore diet of exclusively Christian nonfiction. Virtually every classic I read comes with an introductory essay—sometimes running to a hundred pages—by a contemporary scholar or expert on how to read this particular classic. The Christian book market is now following suit with Karen Swallow Prior's guides to reading great literature.

There is nothing necessarily wrong with all of this, except the danger that we could spend all our time reading about reading and therefore miss out on the pleasure of reading what we first intended to read. This is often a challenge for the Christian—we can be prone to reading books about the Bible (like this one) instead of actually reading our Bible. On the other hand, these guides can often help us see things correctly and aid us in avoiding common pitfalls. As a novice to classic fiction, I often appreciate the accompanying introductions that help readers more clearly see the main themes and narrative trajectories. Learning how to read literature is undoubtedly useful. This has been the aim of this book: helping us learn how to read the Old Testament as Christian Scripture—particularly with the resurrection in mind.

In Mark 12:24–27 Jesus rebukes the Sadducees, an elite and aristocratic Jewish group, for failing properly to understand their Bible. He told them that they knew neither the Scriptures nor the power of God, for they denied the resurrection. This denial is what separated them most sharply from the Pharisees. As I have attempted to elucidate, the resurrection is a constant, though subtle, thread running throughout the Old Testament—the Sadducees' Bible. My prayer is that you and I alike, reader, will grasp both the Scriptures and the power of God as we see Easter in the Old Testament. I trust this book has helped us learn a little better how to read our Bibles properly.

Believing All That Is Stated in the Scriptures

We have taken our lead from Paul on reading resurrection in the Old Testament, and particularly his suggestive phrase in 1 Cor 15:4 that Jesus was "raised on the third day in accordance with the Scriptures." But this is not the only place that Paul makes this argument. Although employing a different vocabulary and being found in a different setting, Paul makes a similar argument in Acts 24.

In Acts 23 Paul is brought before the Jewish council to answer for all that he has been preaching. Knowing that the council consists of Pharisees who believe in the resurrection and Sadducees who do not, Paul claims that it is with respect to the resurrection that he is on trial (22:30—23:6). This caused dissension and debate within the council, which resulted in Paul's being slipped out by the Romans and sent to the Roman governor, Felix. In Acts 24, Paul then finds himself before Felix arguing his case against the high priest, Ananias. It is in the course of defending himself that Paul says more about the resurrection.

Paul happily confesses that "according to the Way, which they call a sect, I worship the God of our fathers, believing everything laid down by the Law and written in the Prophets, having a hope in God, which these men themselves accept, that there will be a resurrection of both the just and the unjust" (24:14–15). Paul's argument, quite simply, is that his hope is the same as that of the Jews who are persecuting him. Just like the Jews, Paul worships the God of the Old Testament, believes the teaching of the Old Testament, and hopes for the resurrection of the Old Testament. Paul is as much a man of the Scriptures as the Jews. The Way, Paul is saying, is simply a continuation of the Old Testament's teachings.

All Paul communicates in these couple of verses demonstrates that the Old Testament is Christian Scripture. This is what the earliest Christians read, preached, prayed, and believed. The significance of this is not merely that resurrection is mentioned in the Old Testament, but that it is *the hope* Paul has in God. From the Law to the Prophets—that is, from the beginning to the end of Paul's Bible—the resurrection is the hope that emerges. This is what he reads and this is what he believes. The whole reason Paul found himself standing before Felix that day is because he came to believe in resurrection from the dead after reading his Bible—the Old Testament.

There is no detailed record of the particular passages Paul had in mind as he took his stand before Felix or wrote his letter to the Corinthians. My proposal is that it could include, but is in no way limited to, the passages we have explored in this brief book. Perhaps Paul saw resurrection power in the creation narrative in Genesis, in Moses's song in Deut 32, and in Hannah's prayer in 1 Sam 2. Is it then possible that Paul followed this up by considering resurrection precursors as both Elijah and Elisha witness the dead being brought back to life by way of resuscitation? These observations might then have caused Paul to linger over resurrection allusions like David following his son in 2 Sam 12, Job anticipating seeing God face-to-face in the flesh after death in Job 19, and the "resurrection" of Jonah from the fish after three days. Did Paul then recite some resurrection poems in praise of the God who delivers from death? Considering all this it would not be surprising if, when Paul told Felix he believed everything written in the Prophets, he was thinking of Ezek 37, Hos 6 and 13, Isa 25–27, and Dan 12. Although I am speculating about the particular passages Paul may have had in mind, it is not speculative to say that there are many to choose from. It is not simply that the Old Testament contains enough proof texts to sustain the doctrine of resurrection, however. No! Resurrection so permeates the Old Testament that resurrection becomes a foundational block in the theological perspective formed by it. In other words, the Old Testament contains, cultivates, and cherishes resurrection hope. This too was Paul's testimony before Felix—he believed all that is stated in the Scriptures.

Embodied in Jesus

Paul did not only read about the resurrection in the Old Testament. He saw it embodied in Jesus (1 Cor 15:8). The real, historical God-man, Jesus of Nazareth, was raised from the dead. In Gal 1:1 we learn that the Father raised him. In Rom 8:11 we learn that the Spirit raised him. In John 10:18 we learn that the Son raised himself. The Trinity worked in perfect harmony exerting resurrection power and ensuring that Jesus of Nazareth walked out of the tomb. In fact, a New Testament resurrection precursor revealed this power before it was exerted. Jesus stands at Lazarus's tomb—where Lazarus had been lying dead for four days—and commands him to come out. He does. This is possible only because Jesus is the resurrection and the life (John 11:25). This resuscitation of Lazarus demonstrates the truth that Jesus is who he says he is.

Even allusions to the unseen are embodied in Jesus. In Luke 24 the disciples on the road to Emmaus are blind to who this man is and what that means about his body. Blind, that is, until Jesus reveals himself as the resurrected Messiah. The same thing happens in John 20 with Mary Magdalene outside the tomb. Embodied in Jesus is all of which the resurrection poems sing: he is delivered from death, made to live, does so in the presence of God—for he is ascended and seated at the Father's right hand—and is imperishable. Jesus is the Davidic king who sees no corruption. Jesus likewise embodies the resurrection prophecies we noted. He is victorious over death, he has awoken from the dust, and the earth has birthed him as the first resurrected son among many.

As Paul has written, Jesus is raised according to the Scriptures. All of the facets of resurrection hope we have noted in the Old Testament are embodied in Jesus.

Knowing the Scriptures and the Power of God

Every time I read Luke 24 I am forced to pause. I am struck by the fact that when the disciples failed to comprehend the events that transpired over the previous days in Jerusalem Jesus himself pointed them to the Scriptures. Jesus could have performed a miracle or, as he later did, revealed who he was by opening their eyes. But he did not. Instead, he interpreted to them all the things in the Scriptures concerning himself (Luke 24:27). He pointed them to the Bible.

Jesus wants his disciples to know the Scriptures. The overarching goal of this book has been to equip us to know the Scriptures better, particularly by learning how to read the Old Testament as Christian Scripture. We are attempting to follow Jesus's example. And while I make no claim to teach with the authority of Jesus Christ, I do pray that your heart has burned within you as we have explored resurrection in the Old Testament. What we call the Old Testament is, after all, the majority of our Bible and we should know it better than we do.

One of the key reasons for knowing the Scriptures is because through them we know the power of God. A power, Paul tells us, that is contained in the gospel (Rom 1:16). The good news about Jesus Christ is the power of God. That good news includes the resurrection. Seeing this, knowing this, believing this helps us see, know, and believe the power of God. In Jesus we see all that the Old Testament pointed to for us and promised to us. In knowing the Scriptures we know the power of God because we come to know Jesus.

The importance of growing in the grace and knowledge of our Lord Jesus Christ becomes apparent in understanding that we will follow him. He is the firstborn among the dead. He is the author of our salvation. He is the older brother in whose footsteps we follow. And so, as we see Old Testament resurrection hope embodied in Jesus we come to John's realization that according to the Scriptures Jesus must rise from the dead (John 20:9). Indeed, he did. Resurrection is the culmination of Old Testament hope and so after reading the Scriptures we come to the assurance that we too must rise from the dead. This is Easter in the Old Testament.

For Further Study

IF YOUR HEART HAS burned within you and you want to delve more deeply into resurrection hope in the Old Testament, I recommend beginning with the below resources.

Blog Posts

Matthew Barrett, "The Resurrection of Christ in the Old Testament." *Credo*, https://credomag.com/2013/03/the-resurrection-of-christ-in-the-old-testament/.

Mitchell L. Chase, "Does the Old Testament Teach Resurrection Hope?" *The Gospel Coalition*, https://www.thegospelcoalition.org/article/old-testament-teach-resurrection-hope/

Justin Dillehay, "How the Old Testament Prepares Us for the Third Day." *The Gospel Coalition*, https://www.thegospelcoalition.org/article/old-testament-third-day/.

S. D. Ellison, "Anticipating Easter in the Old Testament." *The Gospel Coalition*, https://www.thegospelcoalition.org/article/easter-old-testament/.

Herald Gandi, "The Resurection: 'According to the Scriptures'?" *The Master's Seminary Blog*, https://blog.tms.edu/resurrection-according-to-scriptures.

Books

Mitchell L. Chase, *Resurrection Hope and the Death of Death*. Short Studies in Biblical Theology, Crossway, 2022, 176 pages.

N. T. Wright, *The Resurrection of the Son of God*. Christian Origins and the Question of God 3, SPCK, 2003/2017, 848 pages.

Journal Articles

Mitchell L. Chase, "The Genesis of Resurrection Hope: Exploring Its Early Presence and Deep Roots." *Journal of the Evangelical Theological Society* 57.3 (2014) 467–80.

———. "'From Dust You Shall Arise': Resurrection Hope in the Old Testament." *The Southern Baptist Journal of Theology* 18.4 (2014) 9–29.

Stephen G. Dempster, "From Slight Peg to Cornerstone to Capstone: The Resurrection of Christ on 'The Third Day' according to the Scriptures." *Westminster Theological Journal* 76.2 (2014) 371–409.

Jason S. DeRouchie, "Why the Third Day? The Promise of Resurrection in All of Scripture." *Midwestern Journal of Theology* 20.1 (2021) 19–34.

Joel R. White, "'He was Raised on the Third Day according to the Scriptures' (1 Corinthians 15:4): A Typological Interpretation Based on the Cultic Calendar in Leviticus 23." *Tyndale Bulletin* 66.1 (2015) 103–19.